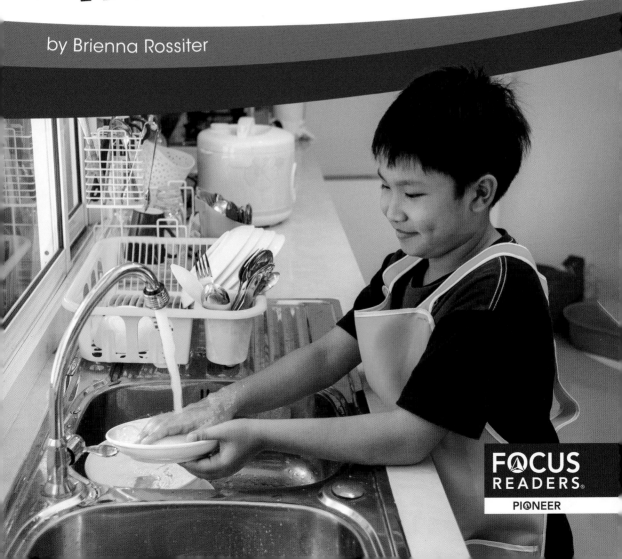

Spreading Kindness

Helping with Chores

by Brienna Rossiter

FOCUS READERS

PIONEER

www.focusreaders.com

Focus Readers is distributed by North Star Editions: sales@northstareditions.com | 888-417-0195

Produced for Focus Readers by Red Line Editorial.

Photographs ©: Shutterstock Images, cover, 1, 8, 10, 12, 18, 21; iStockphoto, 4, 6, 14, 17

Library of Congress Cataloging-in-Publication Data
Names: Rossiter, Brienna, author.
Title: Helping with chores / by Brienna Rossiter.
Description: Lake Elmo, MN : Focus Readers, 2021. | Series: Spreading
  kindness | Includes index. | Audience: Grades 2-3
Identifiers: LCCN 2020033519 (print) | LCCN 2020033520 (ebook) | ISBN
  9781644936856 (hardcover) | ISBN 9781644937211 (paperback) | ISBN
  9781644937938 (pdf) | ISBN 9781644937570 (ebook)
Subjects: LCSH: Families--Juvenile literature. | Chores--Juvenile
  literature. | Helping behavior--Juvenile literature. |
  Kindness--Juvenile literature.
Classification: LCC HQ744 .R674 2021 (print) | LCC HQ744 (ebook) | DDC
  306.85--dc23
LC record available at https://lccn.loc.gov/2020033519
LC ebook record available at https://lccn.loc.gov/2020033520

Printed in the United States of America
Mankato, MN
012021

About the Author

Brienna Rossiter is a writer and editor who lives in Minnesota. She loves cooking food and being outside.

Table of Contents

Chapter 1

You Can Help

Chores are jobs that people do regularly around the home. Chores keep the space clean and nice to live in. Helping with chores shows others that you care.

For example, you can help in the kitchen. You can help cook or **prepare** food. Or you can help do the dishes. You can wash them and put them away. You can also take out the trash.

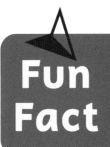

Fun Fact

Some people eat with plates and forks. Others use chopsticks and bowls.

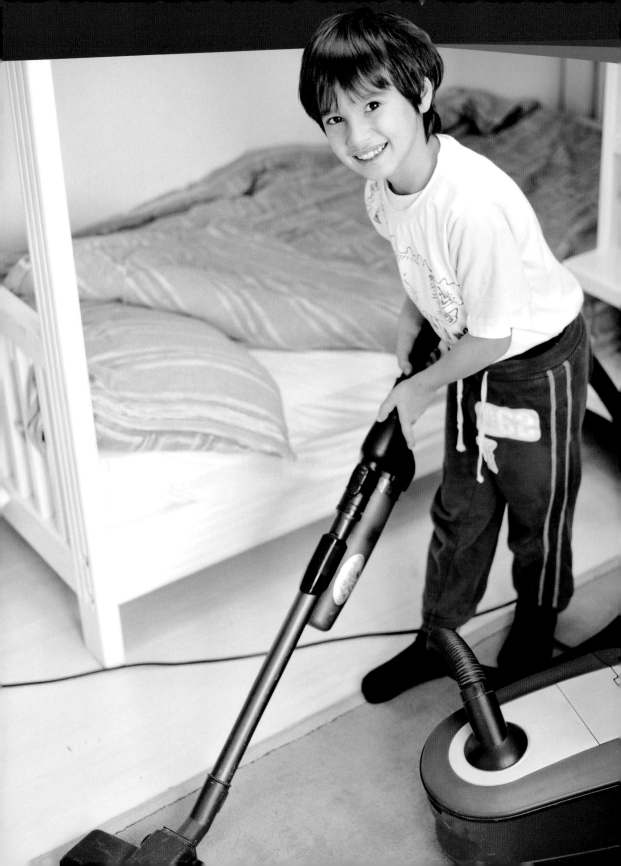

Chapter 2

Cleaning

Many chores involve cleaning. For example, you can help clean the floor. You can use a broom to sweep. You can **vacuum** rugs or carpet.

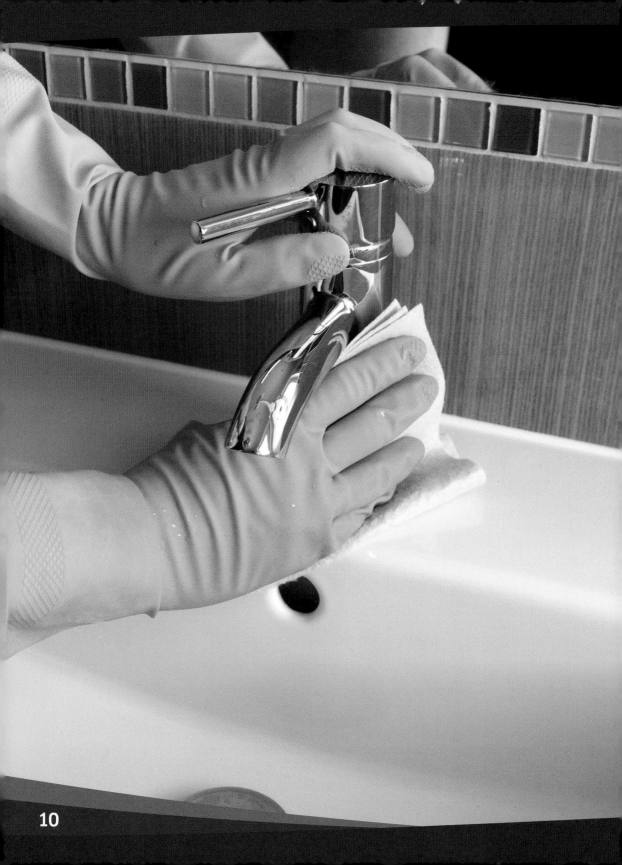

You can clean the kitchen or bathroom. Use a rag and soapy water. Wipe down the sink and counters. Clean the shower or bathtub, too.

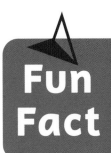

Fun Fact

Cleaning the kitchen is important. The sink can have more **germs** than a toilet!

Chapter 3

Laundry

Another chore is doing laundry. Gather dirty clothes, sheets, and towels. Sort them into piles. Then put them in the washing machine. You can also help dry them or hang them up.

After the laundry is dry, fold the sheets and towels. Sort the clothes. Then help put them away. Bring them to a **dresser** or closet.

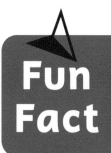

Fun Fact

People **iron** some clothes. The heat gets rid of wrinkles in the fabric.

Make the Bed

You can help put sheets on a bed. A fitted sheet goes first. Pull the stretchy parts around the bed's corners. A flat sheet goes next. Then add blankets. Let part of them hang off the end of the bed. Tuck this part under the **mattress**. Then place the pillow at the other end.

Chapter 4

Other Chores

You can help keep other spaces clean. Pick up toys that are out on the floor. Put them back where they belong.

You can even help outside. You might rake leaves. You might weed a garden. Or you might shovel snow.

By paying attention, you can notice what needs to be done. Then you can **volunteer** to help.

More Chores

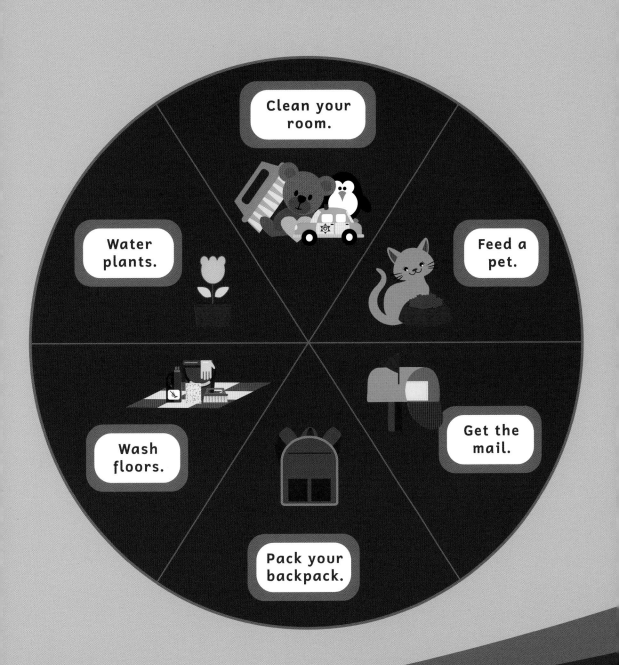

Clean your room.

Water plants.

Feed a pet.

Wash floors.

Get the mail.

Pack your backpack.

FOCUS ON
Helping with Chores

Write your answers on a separate piece of paper.

1. Write a sentence describing one chore you can do in the kitchen.

2. What chore do you think is the easiest to do? What makes it so easy?

3. What is one chore that people do outside?
- A. wash the dishes
- B. weed a garden
- C. vacuum a floor

4. What would happen if people stopped doing chores?
- A. The home would get very messy.
- B. The home would be cleaner.
- C. The home would fall down.

Answer key on page 24.

Glossary

dresser
A place where people put clean clothes.

germs
Tiny living things that can cause illness.

iron
To press a hot, metal tool over fabric. This tool helps smooth out wrinkles.

mattress
A soft pad that people sleep on.

prepare
To make something ready to be used.

vacuum
To clean with a tool that sucks up dust and dirt.

volunteer
To do something without being asked and without being paid.

To Learn More

BOOKS

Huddleston, Emma. *Cooking a Meal.* Lake Elmo, MN: Focus Readers, 2021.

Mach, Jo Meserve, and Vera Lynne Stroup-Rentier. *Cooper Wants to Help with Chores.* Topeka, KS: Finding My Way Books, 2019.

NOTE TO EDUCATORS

Visit **www.focusreaders.com** to find lesson plans, activities, links, and other resources related to this title.

Index

Answer Key: **1.** Answers will vary; **2.** Answers will vary; **3.** B; **4.** A